Conrad K. Butle

Construction machines
FOR KIDS

Articulated dumper

it is a very large and heavy tipper used for transporting loads in difficult terrain and occasionally on public roads.

Asphalt paver

it is a machine for spreading, shaping, and partially compacting a layer of asphalt on a road, parking lot, or other areas.

Backhoe loader

combines two popular heavy equipment functions: digging and moving. There is a loader bucket on one side for pushing, lifting, and moving materials, and on the other side is an excavator for easy digging.

Boom lift

a type of lift basket that allows you to reach both horizontally and vertically. Boom arms make it easier than ever to get into tight spots and reach heights.

Bulldozer

it is a large motorized machine equipped with a metal blade at the front to push materials such as sand, snow, rubble, or stones during construction work.

Carry deck crane

they are built to lift material that needs a compact, low-profile crane. Because Carry deck cranes are small, they are ideal when it comes to operating in tight spaces or around overhead obstacles.

Cold planer

is a construction machine used to remove bituminous or asphalt concrete from roads, resulting in a slightly rough and even surface on which a new layer of asphalt can be laid.

Compact track loader

they are essentially skid steer loaders with high flotation rubber tracks, allowing these earthmoving machines to work in poor ground conditions and on delicate surfaces.

Drum roller

it is a vehicle used to compact soil, gravel, concrete, or asphalt in road and foundation construction. Similar rollers are also used in landfills or agriculture.

Excavator

an earthmoving machine for separating debris from the ground and transferring it by means of transport or to a landfill. The bulldozer can also function as a reloading device.

Feller buncher

a type of harvester used in logging. It is a motorized vehicle with an attachment that can quickly collect and cut down a tree before felling it.

Forklift

it is a small industrial vehicle, which has
an electrically powered forked platform
attached at the front that can be raised
and lowered to insert under a load
for lifting or moving.

Forwarder

a tractor for skidding short timber (logs and rollers) used in forestry. It is a self-loading machine. The wood is loaded into the machine with the help of a crane and does not come into contact with the ground during skidding.

Forest harvester

it is a multi-operational machine. It is currently one of the most technologically advanced wood harvesters.

Knuckleboom loader

as a type of rotating equipment, knuckle boom loaders have a boom strategically designed for log handling applications.

Motor Grader

earthmoving machine, used mainly for profiling the ground under the surface of roads, airports, ditches, and roadsides, and leveling embankments. They are also used for mixing road materials, removing old surfaces, and for leveling the surface of the field.

Scissor lift

a work platform that can only move in the vertical plane on which personnel, equipment, and materials can be raised to perform work.

Skid-steer loader

it is a small, rigid, engine-driven machine with lift arms that can be attached to a wide variety of buckets and other low-maintenance work tools or attachments.

Skidder

it is a piece of heavy machinery that removes cut trees from a forest. Almost all versions of the skidder today have heavy-duty tires or tracks and can move a larger number of trees.

Telescopic handler

they are versatile machines that lift, move and place material. On these job sites, workhorses are often the first machines on the job and the last to leave because they can be used for so many different applications.

Trencher

they are like a bulldozer in that they serve the same purpose of breaking up soil and rock and pulling them out of the ground. However, unlike bulldozers, trenchers can remove soil in one continuous motion.

Wheel tractor-scraper

it is a type of heavy earthmoving equipment. It has a tray/hopper for loading and transporting material. It is most often used during earthworks on road investments.

Check also:

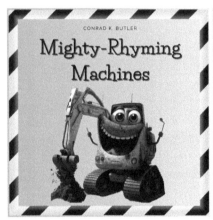

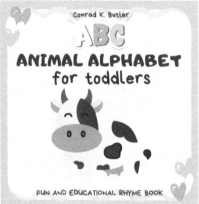

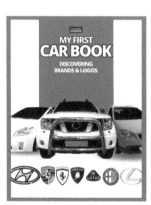

and much more!

 /conradpublishing

Printed in the USA
CPSIA information can be obtained
at www.ICGtesting.com
LVHW070342161023
761186LV00041B/815